DEVELOPMENT
FIRST
WORKBOOK

—

*Creating Your Own
Learning Plan*

Personnel Decisions International Corporation
2000 Plaza VII Tower, 45 South Seventh Street
Minneapolis, MN 55402-1608
USA

Cover design by Deborah Wischow
Text design by Elizabeth Weixel

PDI books are available at special discounts for bulk purchases by corporations, institutions, and other organizations. For more information, please contact Client Relations at Personnel Decisions International Corporation, 2000 Plaza VII Tower, 45 South Seventh Street, Minneapolis, MN 55402-1608, or call 800.633.4410 or 612.904.7170.

Web site: www.personneldecisions.com.

ISBN: 0-938529-21-8

Contents

Create a Learning Plan

Welcome to the *Development FIRST Workbook*. We hope that using it makes your development journey easier and more rewarding. The ability to learn quickly is one of the most important skills you can develop; this workbook is a practical tool to help you learn what you need to know.

In a constantly changing business world, the amount of what you must know and learn can be overwhelming. What skills and capabilities will you need within the next year? Within five years? Over the course of your career? To prepare for what lies ahead, you need to develop your abilities in as short a time as possible.

The purpose of this workbook is to help you begin your development by creating a learning plan that is clear, focused, and realistic. It is based on the book *Development FIRST: Strategies for Self-Development* by David B. Peterson and Mary Dee Hicks (Personnel Decisions International, 1995). *Development FIRST* contains an in-depth, engaging discussion of the development process contained in this workbook.

In part one of the workbook, you will learn how to create a learning plan. In part two, you will learn how to work through your learning plan as you continue the development process.

As you work on your learning plan:

You will:

- Collect and discuss performance feedback.

- Work with your manager to identify development priorities.

- Schedule and conduct a development discussion with your manager.

- Draft a learning plan.

- Implement your plan and seek necessary ongoing feedback and support.

Ask your manager to:

- Encourage you as you work on your development.

- Discuss where you stand in your development and what it takes to be successful.

- Commit to meet with you for a development discussion.

- Work with you to identify development priorities.

- Offer you ongoing feedback and support as you work on your development.

Step 1

Understand the Development FIRST® Strategies

The Development FIRST strategies outline five essential elements necessary for learning and using new skills. This part leads you through the first two: Focus and Implement. Part two, on pages 27–31, provides guidance on completing the other three elements as you continue your development. Review these strategies now and apply them in the course of your development to ensure that learning really happens.

Focus on priorities: identify your critical issues and development objectives.

- Focusing on one or two relevant objectives helps you find the energy and resources to make development really happen.
- You can make the most of the talents you already have by leveraging your strengths.
- When you analyze your GAPS, you can choose development objectives that will benefit both you and your organization.

Implement something every day: stretch your comfort zone daily.

- Development objectives and tactics need to be translated into daily action to make change a reality.
- Spending just five minutes every day working on your development can produce noticeable benefits.

Reflect on what happens: extract maximum learning from your experiences.

- You can learn from your successes, mistakes, and emotions.
- Change is more likely to happen when you pause to consolidate and assimilate learning experiences.

Seek feedback and support: learn from others' ideas and perspectives.

- You'll receive relevant information about your progress so you can measure how you are doing against your development objectives.
- With the support of coaches and other resources, you will find it easier to sustain motivation and stay on course.

Transfer learning to the next level: adapt and plan for continued learning.

- Periodically, you need to step back from your learning plan and take stock of your overall progress. You may need to revise your plan or apply new learning in different situations.
- You'll embark on a continuous circle of learning, enabling you to keep your skills sharp.

Step 2

Complete the GAPS Grid

Your development is a journey that will take you from where you are now to where you want to be. By completing the GAPS grid (Goals and values, Abilities, Perceptions, and Success factors), you can begin to map out your path. You will develop a clear picture of what is most important to you and to others, and you'll be able to pinpoint where additional skill development can give you the greatest benefits.

The GAPS grid helps you focus your energy on development objectives that will make a significant difference for both you and your organization. The left column shows where you stand now, and the right column includes those things that matter most to you and to your organization. The top row contains your own thoughts and perspectives, while the bottom row reflects others' viewpoints.

Review the questions in the GAPS grid below. For guidance on completing one of your own, look at the GAPS questions, sources of GAPS information, and sample on the following pages. Also conduct a development discussion with your manager (see page 25). Your manager's input will be valuable as you complete your grid and choose development objectives.

GAPS: Critical Information for Development

	Where you are	Where you are going
Your view	**Abilities** (How you see yourself) What is your view of your own capabilities, style, and performance, especially in relation to important goals and success factors?	**Goals and Values** (What matters to you) What motivates and energizes you? What important interests, values, desires, work objectives, and career aspirations drive your behavior?
Others' views	**Perceptions** (How others see you) How do others perceive you, including your capabilities, style, performance, motives, priorities, and values?	**Success Factors** (What matters to others) What do other people, such as your boss, senior managers, peers, and direct reports expect or desire from you? Consider your formal and informal roles and responsibilities as well as cultural norms and values.

GAPS questions

Answer the following questions as you complete your GAPS grid. It is often helpful to meet with your manager to talk about these questions. A sample completed grid can be found on page 6. You'll find a blank grid to complete on page 7.

	Where you are	**Where you are going**
Your view	**Abilities** • Where have you been most successful? What skills have contributed to your success? • Where have you been least successful? What additional skills would have been helpful for you? • Based on performance appraisals and your own perceptions of your track record, what do you see as your abilities? • In what areas do you turn to others for assistance? • In what areas are you most likely to offer expertise to others?	**Goals and Values** • What are your most important goals, values, and interests? • What do you want to do that you are not doing now? • What's most important to you? What do you care about most in your work and your life? • In what ways do you want to contribute at work? What do you hope to accomplish? • What gives you the greatest sense of satisfaction and reward?
Others' views	**Perceptions** • Based on feedback from others, how do you think other people see you? • What do others say about your strengths and development needs? • What is your reputation with different groups and at different levels of the organization? • What feedback have you received that you disagree with?	**Success Factors** • What are the expectations and criteria for success in your current position? • What expectations are placed on you because of the company's culture? • Who is most valued and respected in the organization? Why? • What do your supervisors and senior management value most from you? • What capabilities are in greatest demand at the organization right now? Which ones will be most important in the future?

Sources of GAPS information

The following sources can help you find the information you need to answer the GAPS questions.

	Where you are	Where you are going
Your view	**Abilities** • Self-assessment • Track record • Professional assessment	**Goals and Values** • Development planning • Career development discussions • Personal goal setting • Values clarification
Others' views	**Perceptions** • Direct feedback from others • 360-degree feedback • Customer feedback • Performance reviews	**Success Factors** • Roles and responsibilities • Role models and people that others look up to • Function/role descriptions • Competency models • Organizational vision and values • Organizational strategies and goals • Core competencies • Competitive challenges and market demands

Sample GAPS grid

Here is an example of a completed GAPS grid. Note that the person identified some additional questions to answer as he or she goes through the development process.

	Where you are	Where you are going
Your view	**Abilities** What I already know: • *Good problem solver and writer* • *Very strong project management skills (planning and coordination)* • *Need to be better at building teams (especially informal teams) and working across boundaries* • *I'm not that great at networking.* Issues I still need to address: • *My strategic thinking and group leadership skills have not really been tested.* • *I haven't done much public speaking.*	**Goals and Values** What I already know: • *Continue to find new roles where I can make meaningful contributions* • *Keep learning and facing new challenges* • *Be respected and appreciated for my contributions* Questions I still need to answer: • *Would I like more management responsibility?* • *What is the right balance for me between work and family life?*
Others' views	**Perceptions** What I already know: • *People tell me I'm thorough, detail-oriented, and have great follow-through.* • *I work well independently, am easygoing, and am a good team player in groups.* • *My boss keeps saying, "Take more of a leadership stand, voice your opinions, and be more proactive in trying to influence the group."* Questions I still need to answer: • *What do people think about how I delegate and communicate?* • *What does senior management think of me?*	**Success Factors** What I already know: • *Both quality and quantity of work are critical.* • *Demonstrate initiative.* • *Getting buy-in from others and building momentum seems essential.* Questions I still need to answer: • *How important is it to have cross-functional experience?* • *What skills will be most important in the next few years? What does management think we need most?*

Your GAPS grid

	Where you are	Where you are going
Your view	**Abilities**	**Goals and Values**
Others' views	**Perceptions**	**Success Factors**

Step 3

Identify Potential Development Objectives

This step will help you identify improvement areas that will produce the greatest benefit for you and your organization.

Development objectives can be in three categories. Think about these categories as you mull over the information on your GAPS grid:

- **Knowledge:** What do you need to know to reach your goals or to help the business reach its goals? Example: You may need to better understand your organization's strategy.

- **Skill:** How could you apply your knowledge to your job? What actions can you take to improve the business? Example: You may need to learn how to create an accurate budget.

- **Behavior:** What can you change about your behavior? What do you need to start doing or stop doing? Example: Perhaps you often interrupt people and need to stop.

Also, think about potential development objectives from two perspectives. First, start with your own perspective. For example, you may already be aware of weaknesses you have or skills you'd like to learn. Secondly, consider the organization's perspective. Think about the goals your organization is pursuing and look for knowledge, skills, or behaviors you can develop to help the organization reach its business objectives.

Use the exercise on the following pages to analyze your GAPS grid.

> **1. Identify objectives that are important to both you and the organization.** Analyze the right column of your GAPS grid. Consider points of alignment between your goals and values and the organization's success factors. What could you do that would provide benefits for both of you?
>
> List all the development objectives that you think could benefit you and your organization. You can refer to this list in the future as you choose new development objectives.

1. _____

   _____

2. _____

   _____

3. _____

   _____

4. _____

   _____

5. _____

   _____

6. _____

   _____

7. _____

   _____

8. _____

   _____

9. _____

   _____

10. _____

    _____

> **2. Find gaps between your current knowledge, skills, or behaviors and the goals you want to achieve.** Analyze the left column of your GAPS grid. Consider your abilities and the abilities others see in you. Compare it with your list from the previous page.
>
> Now, analyze the entire grid by comparing the two columns. What are the gaps between where you are now and where you want to be? What may keep you from achieving your goals or the organization's? Identify the development objectives on the previous page that would help you fill in your gaps, and write these below.

_____

_____

_____

_____

_____

_____

_____

_____

_____

_____

_____

_____

_____

_____

_____

_____

3. **Determine the potential difficulty and payback for each development objective.** Then determine which objectives will give you the greatest benefit for your efforts. In the grid below, write each objective you identified on the previous page. Consider:

- Which objectives will be easy for you to attain, and which will be difficult?

- How beneficial will the objective be for you and the organization?

- Which development priorities generate the most payback for a given amount of effort?

	Combined payback to you and your organization		
Difficulty of the objective	Small	Moderate	Substantial
Easy			
Moderate			
Difficult			

Step 4

Select Your Development Objectives

The best objectives are those that are relatively easy to attain but have a big payback. Select the objectives that you are most enthusiastic about and that will most quickly help you meet your personal goals and the organization's expectations.

The most effective development objectives:

- Result in the greatest increase in your overall effectiveness.

- Address issues that occur frequently or consistently.

- Prepare you for new roles or opportunities.

- Increase your job satisfaction.

When you select your development objectives, remember that objectives should be realistic yet challenging; those that are too easy or too hard will not motivate you. You must be comfortable with and committed to each objective.

Now, review the tips for selecting development objectives on the next page. Then, from your list of potential development objectives in Step 3, select one or two that you want to begin working on immediately. Write them below. You will create learning plans for these objectives.

My development objectives (Choose one or two)
1.
2.

Tips for Selecting Development Objectives

Choosing the right objective can make the difference between motivating, fruitful development efforts and frustrating, unproductive attempts. The examples in the right column are not necessarily bad ideas, but they rarely help guide and sustain development action. The examples in the left column connect development with real work requirements and objectives that people care about.

Objectives that lead to meaningful development	Objectives that can lead you astray
1. Changes in knowledge, skills, or behaviors that make a difference at work Be more persuasive with management. *(For someone who aspires to a leadership role.)* Understand our external business environment better. *(For someone who needs to contribute to business strategy.)*	**1. Weaknesses that do not greatly impact the job** Become a dynamic public speaker. *(For someone whose job can be done well without strong public speaking skills.)* Become more strategic in my approach. *(For someone in a nonstrategic role.)*
2. What you must learn to reach the goal Understand the links between finance and marketing so I am ready for my next career move. Learn how to work through others in remote locations so I can handle wider-ranging duties.	**2. Career-related objectives that focus on your goal and not the learning** Complete an MBA so I can get ahead. Get a promotion to the next level.
3. What you would like to change in yourself to achieve desired outcomes Develop better techniques for time management and work efficiency. Learn and apply processes to improve report quality.	**3. Performance measures and business goals** Improve turnaround time by four percent by the end of the year. Eliminate errors in reports.
4. Realistic next steps Build more collaboration in my work group. Consider others' opinions when making decisions.	**4. Grand schemes and generic good intentions** Become a stronger leader. Be a better people person.
5. Improving a skill or capability Resolve conflicts within the team more directly and constructively. Build greater mastery of financial modeling.	**5. Participation in events** Take a course in conflict resolution. Attend a professional association conference.

Step 5

Complete Your Learning Plan

Now that you've identified development objectives, you are ready to complete your learning plan. The plan has a section for each Development FIRST strategy. Read the description of each section, and then complete the learning plans on pages 20–23.

Remember the following guidelines when completing your learning plan:

- Seek help from your manager for development planning ideas and guidance.
- Use one learning plan for each development objective.
- Review the sample learning plan on pages 18–19.
- Refer to the previous grids and exercises.
- Review your plan after you've completed it. It may take a few drafts before you've created a concrete, useful plan that will guide you through your development.

1. FOCUS on priorities

This section has two parts:

Development objective: The skill or behavior you will develop.

Criteria for success: What success on your objectives will look like to you and others. In other words, how you will know that you've accomplished your objective.

Fill in the development objective you identified on page 12. As you write your development objective and criteria for success, keep these points in mind:

- Development objectives should describe a change in behavior, not a business goal.
- Objectives should be specific, measurable (or at least observable), and realistic.

2. IMPLEMENT something every day

This section of the learning plan has three parts: on-the-job action steps, action triggers, and gaining knowledge and skills.

On-the-job action steps: Daily opportunities to practice and build your skills. These are typically on-the-job, real-world activities.

Plan on-the-job activities that will help you practice a specific skill. Identify actions that will push you out of your comfort zone and that you can do often. Since most learning happens in the context of ongoing practice, emphasize real-world experiences.

Plan your development activities and time according to the these proportions:

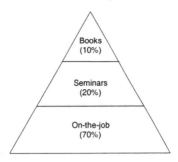

Tips for writing action steps

- Identify when and where you will try the new skill.
- Include an action step to observe someone who effectively uses the new skill, and identify specific things he or she does that might work for you.
- Choose action steps that will challenge you but that are attainable.
- Set realistic target completion dates.
- Ask yourself: What can I do to fine-tune my skills? What different situations or people will help me stretch myself? How do I ensure that I follow through with my action steps?

Action step examples

Objective	Action Step
Keep people up-to-date with information.	Ask my manager, direct reports, and peers to list the information they would like from me. Let them know what I will be able to provide.
Prepare realistic estimates of budget, staff, and other resources.	Review my plans against a like-sized project or initiative.
Analyze problems from different points of view.	Ask coworkers to review my next three project drafts and ask me questions that I may not have considered.

Action triggers: Situations or events that prompt you to practice your new skills. You will complete the statement "Every time I see the following situation(s) . . . ."

Set action triggers that will prompt you to act. Identify common situations in which you can practice the skill, and plan what you will do when you encounter those situations.

Gaining knowledge and skills: Methods to gain a foundation of knowledge or skills.

Note the resources you will need to learn new knowledge or a new skill. For example, books and role models can help you acquire new skills that you can practice on the job.

3. REFLECT on what happens

Reflection is the process of reviewing and learning from your development experiences. As you complete your learning plan, ask yourself how you will think about:

- What worked
- What didn't work
- What you want to continue doing next time
- What you want to do differently next time

Document how you will remember to reflect, when you will do it, and how you will record your thoughts. If necessary, plan a trigger, such as a weekly meeting with your coach, to ensure that you reflect on your learning.

Examples:

- Brian reflects on his way home from work, then leaves himself a voice mail when he arrives home. The next morning, he listens to his message for reminders about his progress and his action steps.
- Juan reflects after events or conversations that surprise him; unexpected events, good or bad, prompt him to review his development.
- Bonnie reflects on her development while she exercises.
- Lin keeps a daily to-do list that reminds her to reflect as she begins her day.
- John makes notes in his personal planner as he is considering the next phase of his projects.
- Carla conducts a debriefing session at the end of every project and team meeting to review how things are working.

4. SEEK feedback and support

This section has two parts:

> *Feedback and information:* How and from whom you will gather feedback about your progress.

> *Support, resources, and opportunities:* How you will get support and development resources from your coach and others.

Plan how you will get the feedback and support you need. Specify:

- Whom you will ask for feedback
- How often you will ask for feedback
- Which events will give you opportunities for feedback
- What kinds of support you need (e.g., time, training, mentoring)

5. TRANSFER learning to the next level

Plan when and how you will review and modify your learning plan. Circumstances change and so do you; your learning plan needs to be flexible to reflect these changes. Schedule times to review your progress and to make changes to your learning plan. Consider how you will take stock of your progress and apply your new skills to other learning opportunities.

Take the time to consider how you can practice your skills and improve your abilities. As you fill out your learning plan, consider how you will:

- Celebrate your accomplishments.
- Continually apply what you've learned.
- Move on to new challenges.

Sample Learning Plan

Name: *Pat Sample*	Date: *April 4*

1. FOCUS on priorities

What is my development priority? What do I want to work on? What skill or behavior do I want to develop or leverage?

Be more effective in influencing peers and higher-level managers, especially about department priorities, strategic direction, and major decisions.

Criteria for success: A brief description of the skill above when performed adequately.

My peers and higher-level managers will seek my advice before making major decisions.

2. IMPLEMENT something every day

Action steps to take to practice my skills	Who to involve	Due date
Select an issue and identify who needs to be influenced.	*Manager*	*5/1*
Develop influence strategy.	*Manager, coach*	*5/15*
Deploy influence strategy and debrief with my manager.	*Manager*	*6/1*

Every time I see the following situation(s) . . . What situations, people, or events signal that now is the time to put new behaviors into action?	. . . I will take the following development action: What new behavior will I try? Where will I push my comfort zone?
1. *Every meeting with peers and higher-level managers where I make a comment or suggestion and then someone else raises a new topic . . .*	1. *Speak up and persist with my idea; ask what others think about my suggestions.*
2. *Every time I feel frustrated or find myself squelching my own opinions in meetings and conversations with peers . . .*	2. *State my position at least one more time and ask for a response or for more information, rather than staying quiet or backing down.*
3. *Every meeting with my team . . .*	3. *Anticipate emerging problems and issues by asking my team for what they see happening. I'll bring relevant issues to my manager with my recommendations for how to respond.*

How will I gain the additional knowledge and skills I need?	Due date
Read the chapter on influence in the Successful Manager's Handbook.	*4/15*
Watch my manager as she influences executives.	*5/15*

3. REFLECT on what happens	
Daily reflection: What will I do each day to consider . . . • What worked? • What didn't work? • What do I want to do differently next time?	◊ *Review my development progress first thing in the morning when I review my calendar for the day.* ◊ *Record insights and questions in my to-do list as they occur, and transfer the most useful ones to my learning log each week following the weekly staff meeting.*

4. SEEK feedback and support	
Feedback and information • How will I track my progress and get input from others? • Who will I ask for feedback? • When?	◊ *Track the number of times my ideas are implemented in the peer group.* ◊ *Ask Carrie and Dale for feedback after each team meeting.* ◊ *Talk to my manager after critical meetings where I'm trying to be influential.*

Support, resources, and opportunities What else do I need to support my learning (e.g., mentors, advocates, contacts, further readings, further training, additional time, etc.)?	**Due date**
Attend an additional training course on influencing skills if I'm not making adequate progress.	*12/1*
Schedule a monthly lunch with people who are good at influencing and who have organizational savvy.	*7/1*
Ask my manager and my mentor for support in getting invited to key meetings, especially on the XYZ project.	*7/15*
In six months, talk to my manager about joining the strategic task force.	*10/1*

5. TRANSFER learning to the next level	
Periodic review • How will I take stock at major milestones to evaluate my progress toward my goals and organizational priorities? • When and how will I evaluate what I need to work on next?	◊ *Review my development progress each quarter at the same time I look at quarterly business results.* ◊ *Discuss my progress and current development priorities with my manager at our quarterly review meeting. Ask for her perceptions and insights.* ◊ *Retake the PDI PROFILOR® 360-degree feedback instrument in one year.*

Your Learning Plan

Name: _____ Date: _____

1. FOCUS on priorities

What is my development priority? What do I want to work on? What skill or behavior do I want to develop or leverage?

Criteria for success: A brief description of the skill above when performed adequately.

2. IMPLEMENT something every day

Action steps to take to practice my skills	Who to involve	Due date

Every time I see the following situation(s) . . . What situations, people, or events signal that now is the time to put new behaviors into action?	. . . I will take the following development action: What new behavior will I try? Where will I push my comfort zone?
1.	1.
2.	2.
3.	3.

How will I gain the additional knowledge and skills I need?	Due date

3. REFLECT on what happens	
Daily reflection: What will I do each day to consider: • What worked? • What didn't work? • What do I want to do differently next time?	

4. SEEK feedback and support	
Feedback and information • How will I track my progress and get input from others? • Who will I ask for feedback? • When?	

Support, resources, and opportunities	Due date
What else do I need to support my learning (e.g., mentors, advocates, contacts, further readings, further training, additional time, etc.)?	

5. TRANSFER learning to the next level	
Periodic review • How will I take stock at major milestones to evaluate my progress toward my goals and organizational priorities? • When and how will I evaluate what I need to work on next?	

Your Learning Plan

| Name: _____ | Date: _____ |

1. FOCUS on priorities

What is my development priority? What do I want to work on? What skill or behavior do I want to develop or leverage?

Criteria for success: A brief description of the skill above when performed adequately.

2. IMPLEMENT something every day

Action steps to take to practice my skills	Who to involve	Due date

Every time I see the following situation(s) . . . What situations, people, or events signal that now is the time to put new behaviors into action?	. . . I will take the following development action: What new behavior will I try? Where will I push my comfort zone?
1.	1.
2.	2.
3.	3.

How will I gain the additional knowledge and skills I need?	Due date

3. REFLECT on what happens

Daily reflection: What will I do each day to consider: • What worked? • What didn't work? • What do I want to do differently next time?	

4. SEEK feedback and support

Feedback and information • How will I track my progress and get input from others? • Who will I ask for feedback? • When?	

Support, resources, and opportunities What else do I need to support my learning (e.g., mentors, advocates, contacts, further readings, further training, additional time, etc.)?	**Due date**

5. TRANSFER learning to the next level

Periodic review • How will I take stock at major milestones to evaluate my progress toward my goals and organizational priorities? • When and how will I evaluate what I need to work on next?	

Critiquing your learning plan

Use the following checklist to evaluate your learning plan.

FOCUS on priorities

- ☐ I have no more than two development objectives.
- ☐ My objectives align with my personal goals and organizational success factors.
- ☐ Objectives are specific, attainable, and stated in behavioral terms.
- ☐ Objectives address areas in which I am motivated and committed to change and develop.
- ☐ I have a good description of what success will look like.

IMPLEMENT something every day

- ☐ My action steps clearly indicate when and where I will take action.
- ☐ The action steps specify exactly what I will do differently.
- ☐ Most of my action steps are on-the-job activities.
- ☐ A variety of activities are included in my action steps.
- ☐ The action steps are challenging but not too difficult.
- ☐ I have realistic target dates for completing the activities and development objectives.

REFLECT on what happens

- ☐ I have described specific and realistic techniques for reflecting on my development.

SEEK feedback and support

- ☐ I have identified people from whom I need support and feedback.
- ☐ I know what specific feedback I need to solicit.
- ☐ I have scheduled progress reviews with my manager.

TRANSFER learning to the next level

- ☐ I have described how I will take stock of my progress.
- ☐ I have planned my next steps.

Conduct a Development Discussion

Meeting with your manager regularly to discuss your development is important. The information below can be used to plan your participation in a development discussion.

Before the meeting

- Contact your manager. Ask him or her to think about areas for development, strengths to leverage, and ideas for action steps.
- Using the GAPS analysis, review what you know about your capabilities.
- Collect a range of input on how others see you (e.g., use 360-degree feedback tools, your performance reviews, other people's direct feedback).
- Review the success factors in your organization.
- Choose one or two development objectives that will benefit you and your organization.
- Draft the first version of a learning plan.
- Identify follow-up questions to clarify feedback you have received.

During the meeting

Collaborate on each step:

- Consider working through a GAPS analysis with your manager. Talk about your goals and abilities. You can add information about others' perceptions and the organization's success factors.
- Talk together about the development objectives you have decided to focus on. Discuss the rationale for choosing them.
- If necessary, negotiate to narrow down the scope of your learning plan. Choose no more than two development objectives.
- Identify development activities and realistic target dates for each objective.
- Consider potential obstacles to development and ways to overcome them.
- Set follow-up meetings.

After the meeting

- Seek ongoing support. Ask your manager to observe your performance and provide feedback.
- Continue to build a trusting relationship with your manager.
- Leverage learning. Create opportunities to practice new skills on the job.

Congratulations!

Completing your learning plan is a major milestone in the development process. However, it is just the first step. The most important effort is yet to come. At this point it is important for you to make a personal commitment to implement your learning plan.

Your new behaviors should become a way of life. They must become part of your normal routine. Be alert for the triggers on your learning plan which are intended to remind you to work on your development objectives. And, as often as possible, schedule activities that will allow you to practice and to reflect on your development progress. Even if it is something small, work on your development each day. By taking many small steps, you will soon make significant progress toward achieving your development objectives.

Continue the Development Process

Development doesn't end with a completed learning plan. It begins. Now you need to act on your learning plan. The following pages provide guidance for working through the development process. Refer to these tips as you progress in your learning.*

FOCUS on priorities

Build on what you know: leverage your strengths

- Gain a greater understanding of your strengths by considering how you would answer the following questions in a job interview:
  - Why should we hire you?
  - What are you skilled at?
  - What special qualities and abilities would you bring to our organization?
  - What things have people praised you for?
- Redefine your current opportunities. First, identify parts of your job that you handle easily. Then add a new challenge by asking yourself:
  - How can I make this more strategic?
  - Can I teach this to others?
  - How can I streamline it and reduce cycle time?
  - How can I make it more effective?
- Benchmark yourself against experts.

IMPLEMENT something every day

Spend just five minutes each day

- Make development routine. Set aside a regular time, such as at the beginning or end of each day, to act and reflect on your development objectives.
- Make your development action step the first task on your daily to-do list.
- Link your goals with something you are already doing. Take a moment each day to identify the development opportunities that are right in front of you.
- Break out of your normal routine. Search for new ways to approach the situations you deal with every day.

---

* Many of these tips come from the *Successful Manager's Handbook* (Personnel Decisions International, 2000), a comprehensive reference book that can help you develop skills in 32 essential areas.

- Learn from your coworkers. Spend time with the people in your department who have the expertise and skills you need. Ask them questions.

- Be flexible and take advantage of opportunities as they arise. Some learning just happens without much planning or forethought.

Make your learning more efficient

- Determine your own most effective learning style. Some people learn best by observation, others by trial and error, and others by reading. Emphasize the style that works best for you.

- Get involved in a variety of experiences to maximize your development. High-quality learning most often comes from a wide range of life activities, not just a few.

- Experiment and take intelligent risks each day. Seek out "high-voltage" situations, such as projects that are highly visible or ones that give you an opportunity to work with new people.

Get the most out of readings and seminars

- Rather than reading an entire book, scan the table of contents to determine which sections are most relevant. Then read just those sections.

- Search for one insight or application in everything you read. Draw conclusions and search for meaning relevant to your development.

- Choose seminars that are relevant to your learning objectives and give you a chance to practice and apply new information and skills.

- Build in time to reflect on and apply what you have learned. Your behavior will not change simply because you have learned something from a book or training program.

Deal with obstacles and roadblocks in your development

- Show your development plans and goals to others. This will increase your commitment to attaining the goals and will involve others in your development. Specifically, ask for support and feedback in the areas you find toughest to master.

- Keep the development process simple. Complexity can make development feel intimidating rather than motivational.

- Do not shy away from discomfort. Accept that change and development may feel frightening or ambiguous at times. Remind yourself that this feeling is only temporary.

- Be patient and realize that change takes time. Real behavioral change feels natural and easy only with persistence and practice.

- Be aware of what happens when your progress begins to slip. Keep track of situations that cause you difficulty and figure out how to address them.

- Redefine success by separating what you are learning from how you are performing. Ask "What have I just learned?" rather than "How did I just do?"

- If you feel stuck or unsuccessful, regroup and correct your course. Revisit your learning plan and make necessary changes in your approach. Review your objectives and actions with others, and seek their candid feedback and advice.

REFLECT on what happens

Regularly reflect on what you have learned

- Schedule periodic reviews, such as at the beginning of each month or quarter, to think about and consolidate what you have learned.

- Use major events, such as the completion of long-term assignments, as opportunities to debrief what went well and what needed improvement.

- Reflect at the midpoint of a large assignment when you still have a chance to make corrections.

- Learn from your successes by examining them and determining exactly what you did to succeed. Then look for opportunities to transfer your behaviors and skills to other situations.

- Tune in to your emotions. Use both positive and negative emotions to motivate you, to draw your attention to something that needs changing, or to identify areas for future growth.

- Consider keeping a learning log to track and document your lessons and progress.

- The next time you work on a development objective, ask yourself, "What have I learned?" Write down what you learned, as well as possible ways to apply your learning to other situations.

- Share your mistakes. Talking through a mistake with others will increase your understanding of the situation. Solicit ideas on what you might do differently in the future.

- If you have not made a mistake lately, ask yourself:
  - Am I challenging myself in my job and outside of work?
  - Am I requesting or hearing feedback from others?
  - Am I taking any risks?

SEEK feedback and support

Seek honest feedback: use the ALERT method

Ongoing feedback is essential for knowing where you are in your development process and for determining your next steps. You need to make a concerted effort to solicit feedback that is honest, concrete, and specific to your development objectives. To make it easier for others to give you the information you need, follow the ALERT method.

1. **Ask for feedback**
   - Explain what you want and why it is important. Describe your learning goals and the topics you are interested in. For example, say "I want to improve my influencing skills. Would you be willing to observe how I am doing in this area?"
   - Convey sincere interest in other people's views. Use statements such as "I need your input because working with you is an important part of my job" or "You've seen me in some tough situations lately, so you may have some valuable observations for me."

- When possible, direct people to pay attention to specific topics and behaviors. For example, say "I'd like you to watch how persuasive I am in the next few staff meetings."
- Make feedback natural by asking for it regularly in your conversations.

2. Listen actively to what people say

- Strive to pursue, understand, and accept other people's points of view.
- Create opportunities for people to expand on what they have said. Use open-ended questions to clarify and probe for examples.
- Resist the urge to argue, explain, or defend yourself.
- Clarify the impact of your behaviors on others. For example, you may ask "What happens when I don't act decisively in our meetings?"

3. Express thanks and reactions

- Reinforce open communication by thanking people for their time and honesty.
- Acknowledge the effort required to share difficult feedback. Statements such as "Thanks for being so candid. You said some tough things that no one else has bothered to tell me" show that you appreciate being told things you need to know.
- Affirm what was most valuable to you, how it made a difference, and what you might do next. For example, try "Thank you for your feedback on my nonverbal behavior. You've given me some issues to think about as I work on my development objectives."
- Keep the lines of communication open. Let people know you would appreciate further conversations. For example, saying "I'm really trying to work on that area. Could we talk again after the next staff meeting?" will establish a specific time to get more feedback.

4. Reflect on what you've heard

Reflect on your:

- *Thoughts*: How does this fit with your goals and your current view of yourself? What new information have you heard? Where do you need additional clarifying information?
- *Feelings*: How do you feel about the conversation (e.g., pleased, concerned, frustrated, angry, satisfied, appreciated)? What surprised you?
- *Actions*: What action is warranted by the feedback you just received? What are your options for taking action? What makes the most sense for you to do next?

5. Take action

- Decide what you want to do next. Plan exactly when and where you will begin.
- Continue to seek feedback to assess your progress.

Build partnerships to bolster your learning

To reach your development goals, good intentions must be translated into action. Most people find that establishing a support system helps them sustain their motivation and continue learning.

- Identify development partners. These are people who have similar development objectives. Development partners can meet for mutual encouragement and accountability.
- Develop a support network. This is an informal group of individuals who will provide input and support for development efforts. These are the significant people in your life who can provide feedback or give advice about development or career planning ideas.
- Find a good mentor who can guide you and hold you accountable.

TRANSFER learning to the next level

Make it count: transfer what you've learned to the next steps

- Take time to celebrate and acknowledge your progress and accomplishments. Personal recognition builds self-confidence and provides renewed energy for your continued growth.
- Create additional opportunities to apply what you have learned. Using your new skills will ensure that you keep them sharp and up-to-date.
- Seek experience in new, complex situations.
- Cross-train and pursue learning in related areas.
- Advance to the next level of mastery. For example, seek experience in a new, complex situation. Force yourself to face additional challenges that will push your limits.
- Take a break to recharge your batteries before your next development challenge. Take stock of what development strategies and tactics worked best so you can apply them in the future.
- Focus on new goals. Update your GAPS grid to include your newly developed skills. Then reanalyze your grid, determine your next development objective, and create a learning plan to help you achieve it.

Notes